Dedication

If my nephews have taught me anything, it's how to make a complete fool of myself and not feel guilty about it. This book is for them. And for my sister, Desiree', who tolerates our nonsense, and to my baby sister, Brittany, who is 100% responsible for the creation of those four little farts who inspired this gleeful **rump** through the mud puddles of immaturity. And to my Mother: Thanks for the **cheeky** sense of humor.

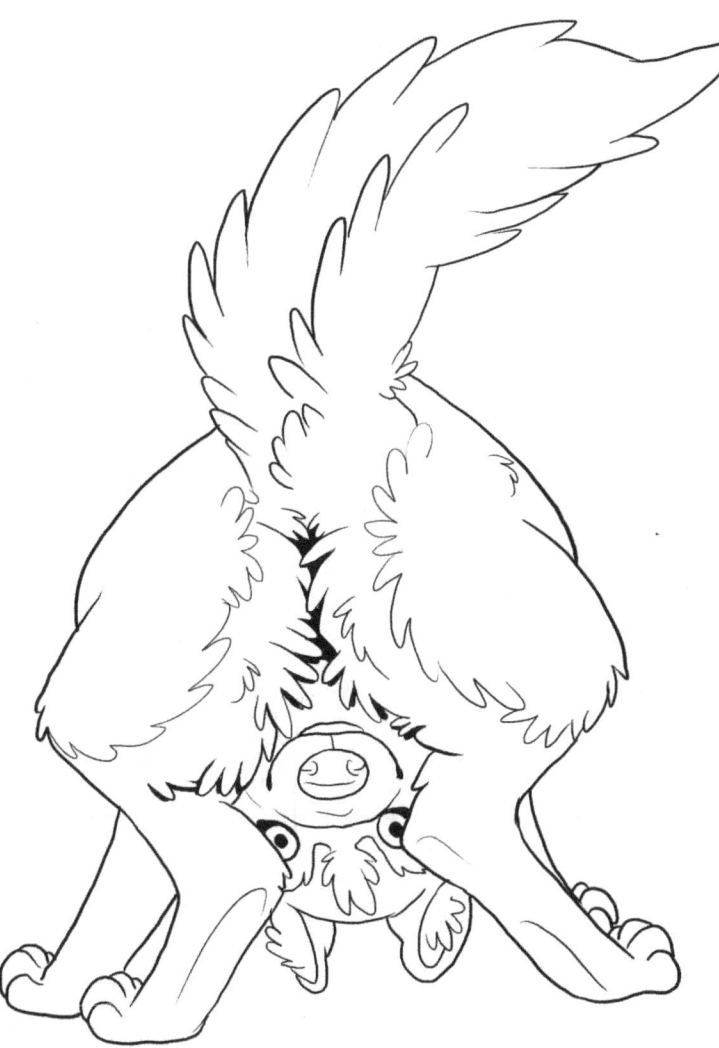

Before we start, let's take a moment to pretend this book might actually boost your IQ by teaching you a few facts about butts.

›››THIS WAY TO FACTS›››

FANNY FACTS

* Glutes are the biggest and strongest muscles in your entire body.

**Some species of turtles have the ability to breathe through their butts.

***The average person farts 13 to 21 times a day.

****"Belfie" is a word for "Butt Selfie"

*****In 2012, a rare species of horse fly was named Scaptia beyonceae, after Beyoncé, because of its gold butt.

BUTT MUSCLES

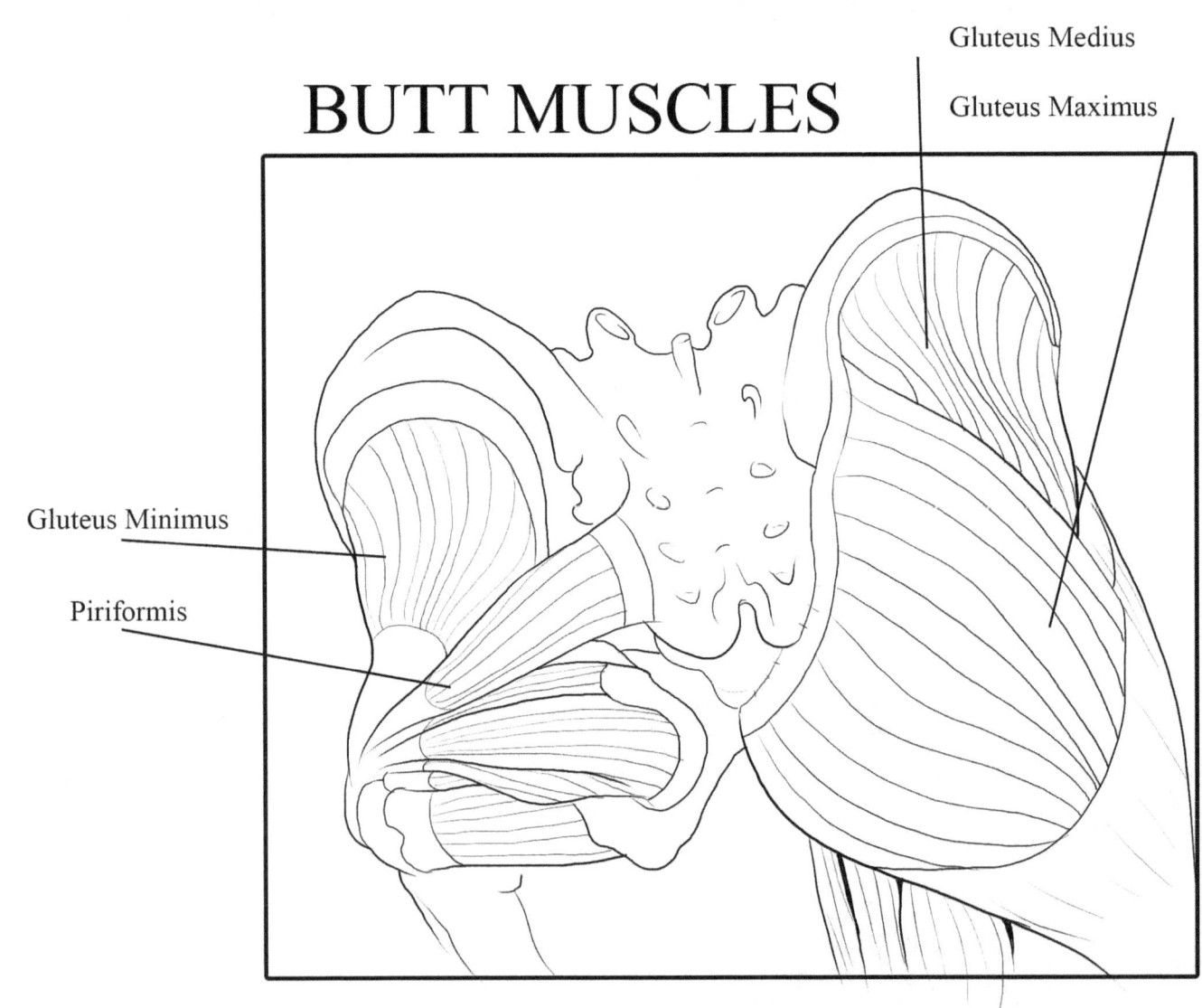

Gluteus Medius

Gluteus Maximus

Gluteus Minimus

Piriformis

RUMP ROMP WORD SEARCH

```
O B U T G V R S F S B M D L W
V X B S U E I T K A J V Y T R
W W F O T S Q S D C J W M T B
F G Z S T A H O D E O K J U J
B J I Z L T N F P Q B T Y B N
K E E H C K O M N P O R T N B
K S M Y A E U M J F O D U U Q
E X N D T R O I R E T S O P B
L W O O R E A R T Q Y M B T E
N N K Z U I S B G Q L O E Y N
K U L F X R W F U T Y W S G Y
S Q O H E R J J F X Z N I X B
A A U Z U E O B B E H I N D P
Q T G A W D A X Z J S T B A U
T T R C M W S B Q Q C E T F F
```

BADONKADONK
BEHIND
BOOTY
BOTTOM
BUTT
BUTTOCKS
CHEEK
DERRIERE
FANNY
KEISTER
POSTERIOR
REAR
RUMP
TOKUS
TUSH

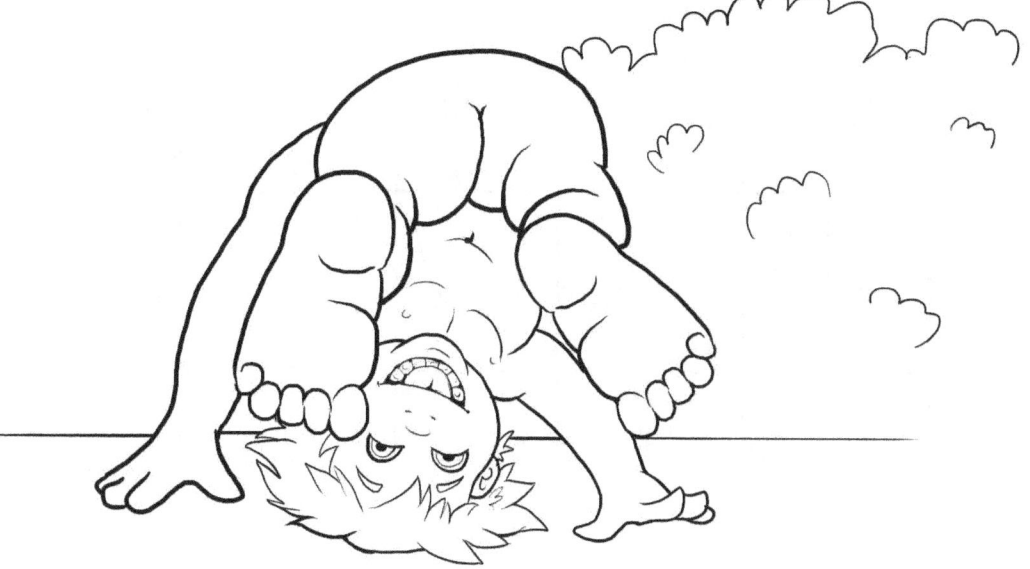

DRAWING BACKTIVITIES

Skinny Minnie

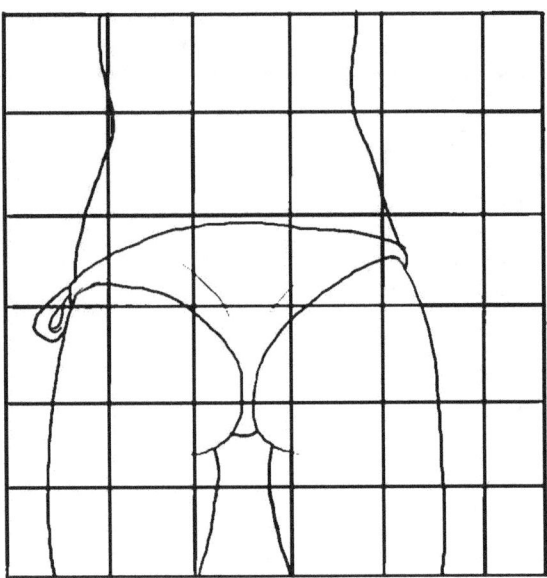

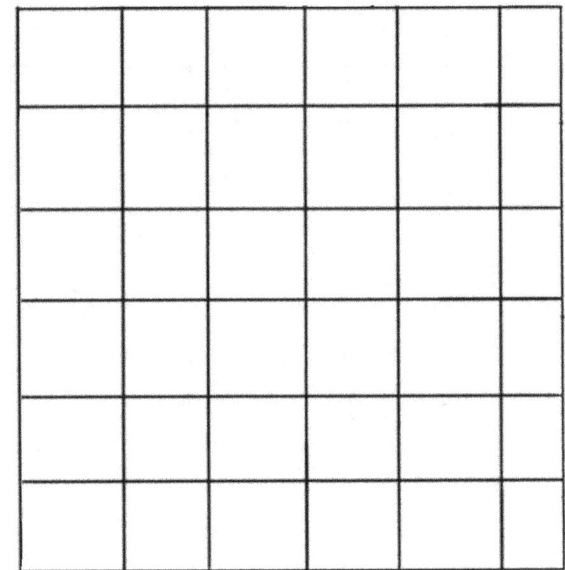

Bunny Buns

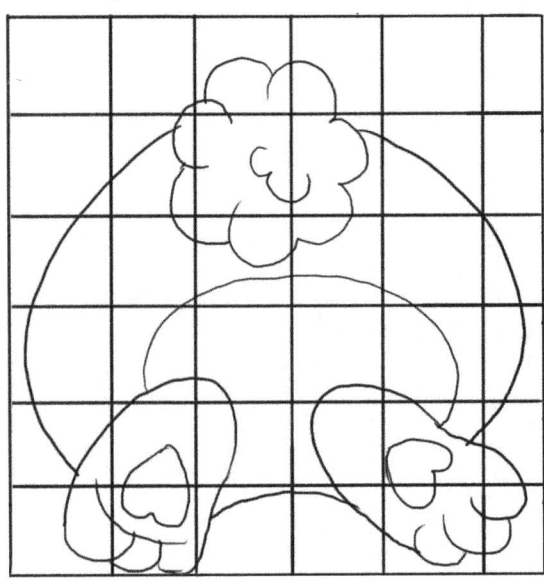

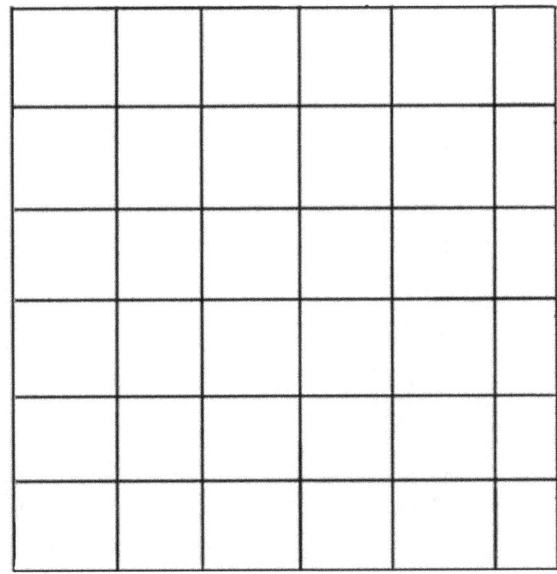

"I hope your **day** is as **nice** as your **butt**"

NOTHING BUT BUTTS
CROSSWORD PUZZLE

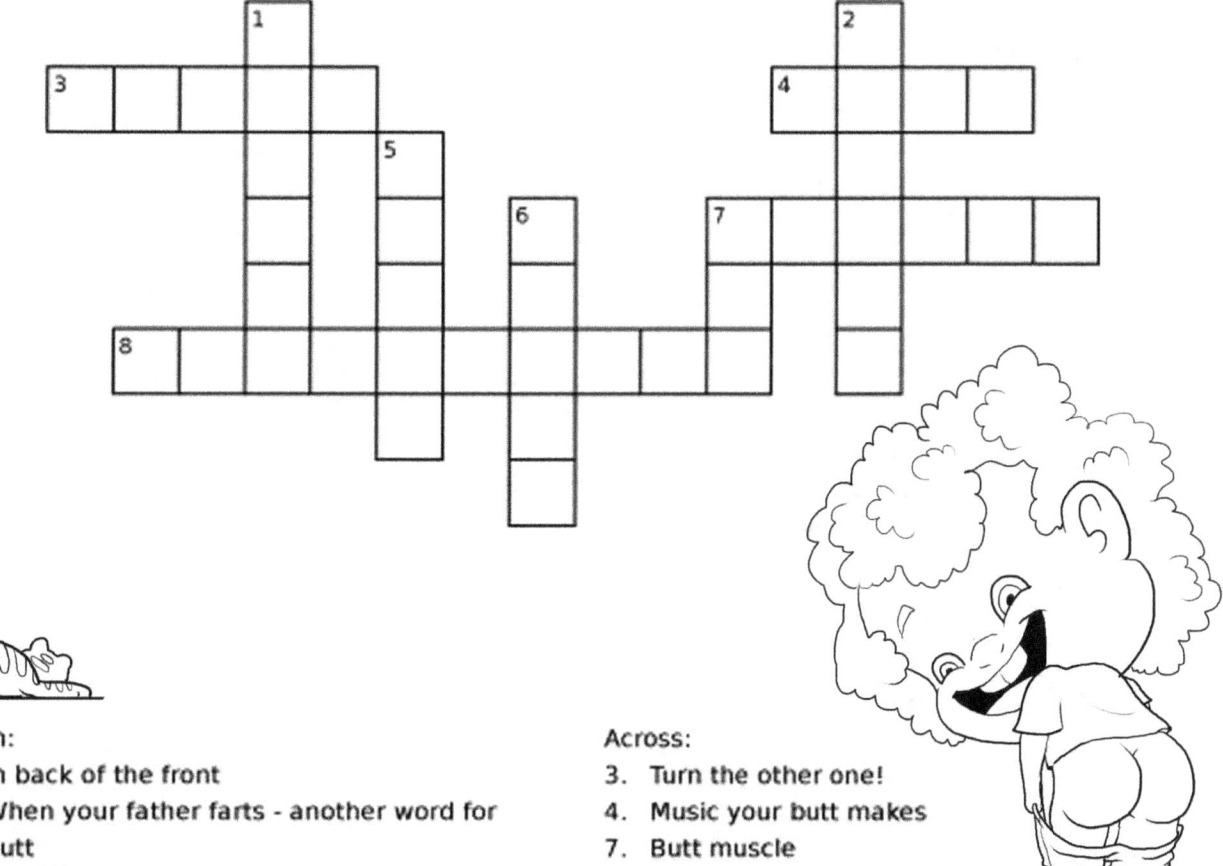

Down:
1. In back of the front
2. When your father farts - another word for butt
5. butt dance
6. Musical fruit
7. Stinky fuel

Across:
3. Turn the other one!
4. Music your butt makes
7. Butt muscle
8. Butt cover

MY POSTERIOR
How many words can you make using the letters found in thie above statement? Write them below:

POOPY PUZZLE

Match the dookie to the bootie it came from.

1 GOLDFISH

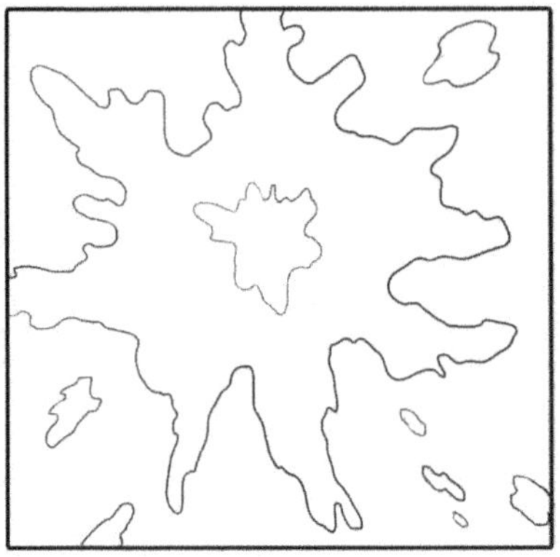

2 COON

3 COW

4 BIRD

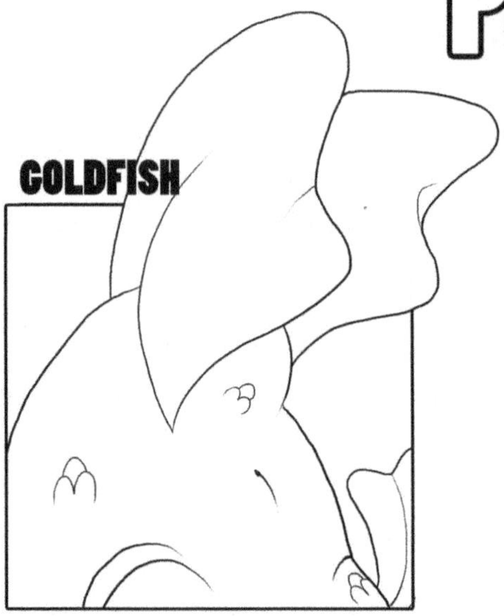

1

2

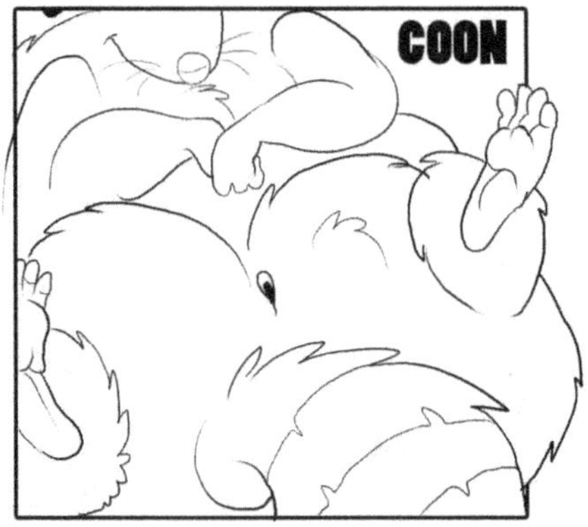

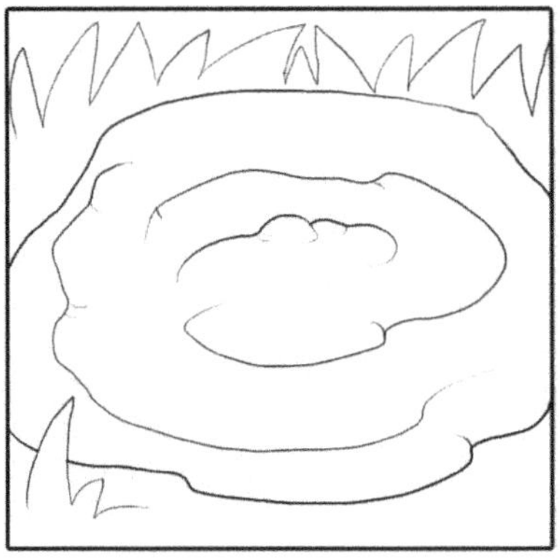

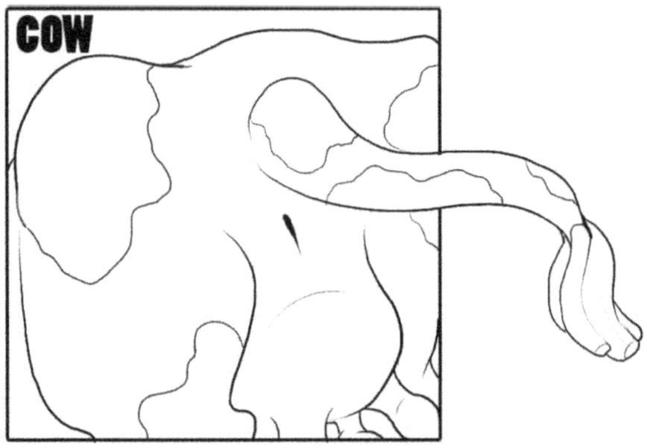

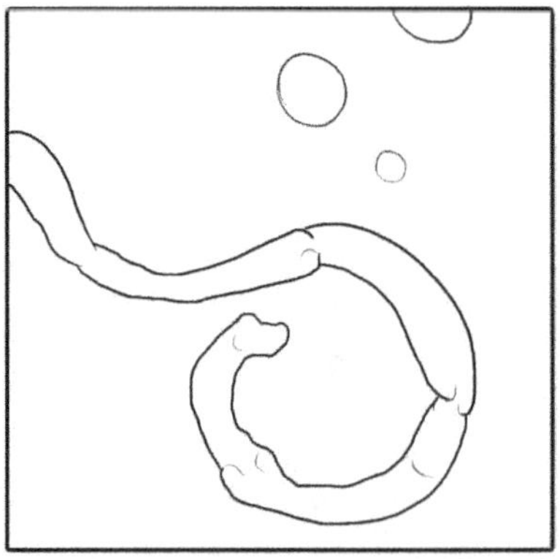

3

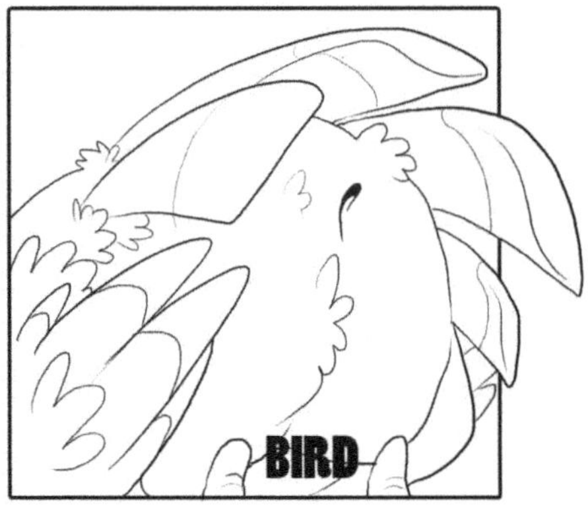

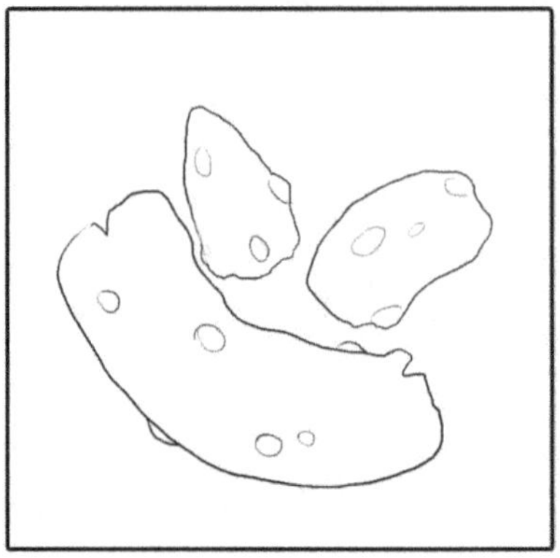

4

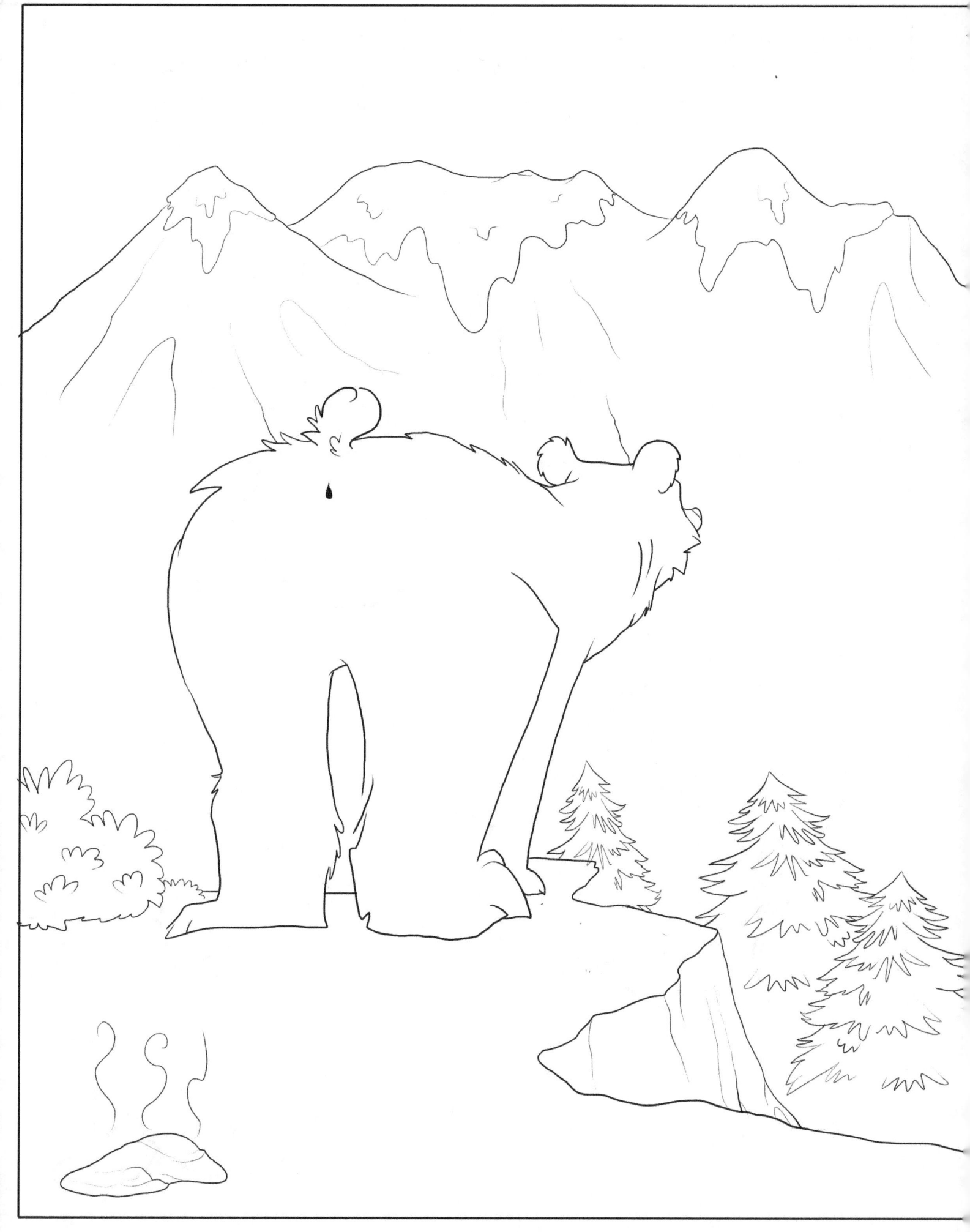

BUTTerflies

haunches rump cheeks backside

POTTY KEISTER

TUSHY BUTTOCKS

FANNY

boop MOON DERRIERE PANTIES

BIKINI REAR

UNDERWEAR CAN TWERK

breech seat

CABOOSE

UNDERWEAR BIGBUTT FART RUMP DIAPER bottom

end Badonkadonk

CHEEKS FART

patoot behind bottom

HEINIE posterior

hams bum SEAT

keister HAIRY kabump

tush buns

duff butt derriere

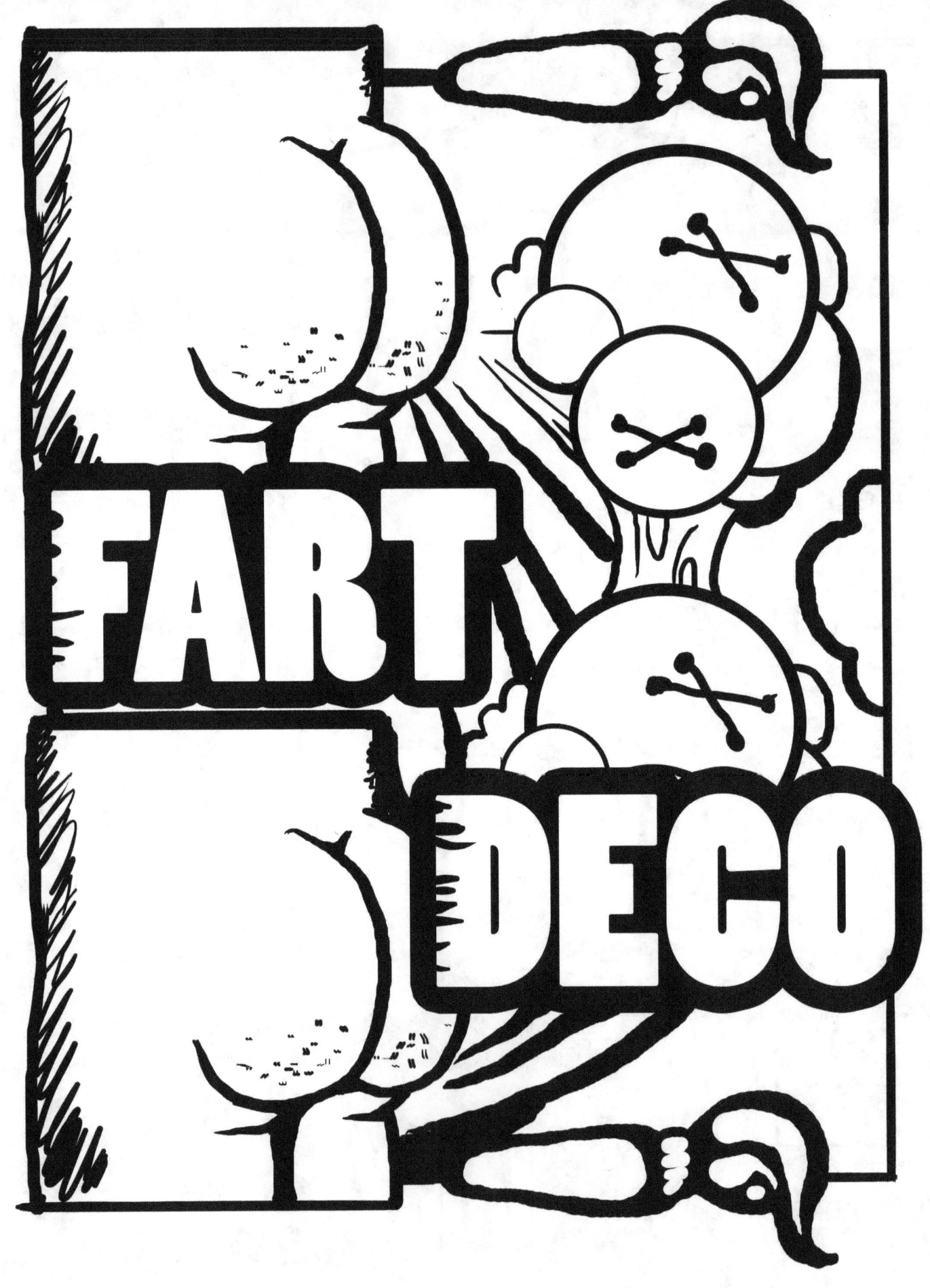

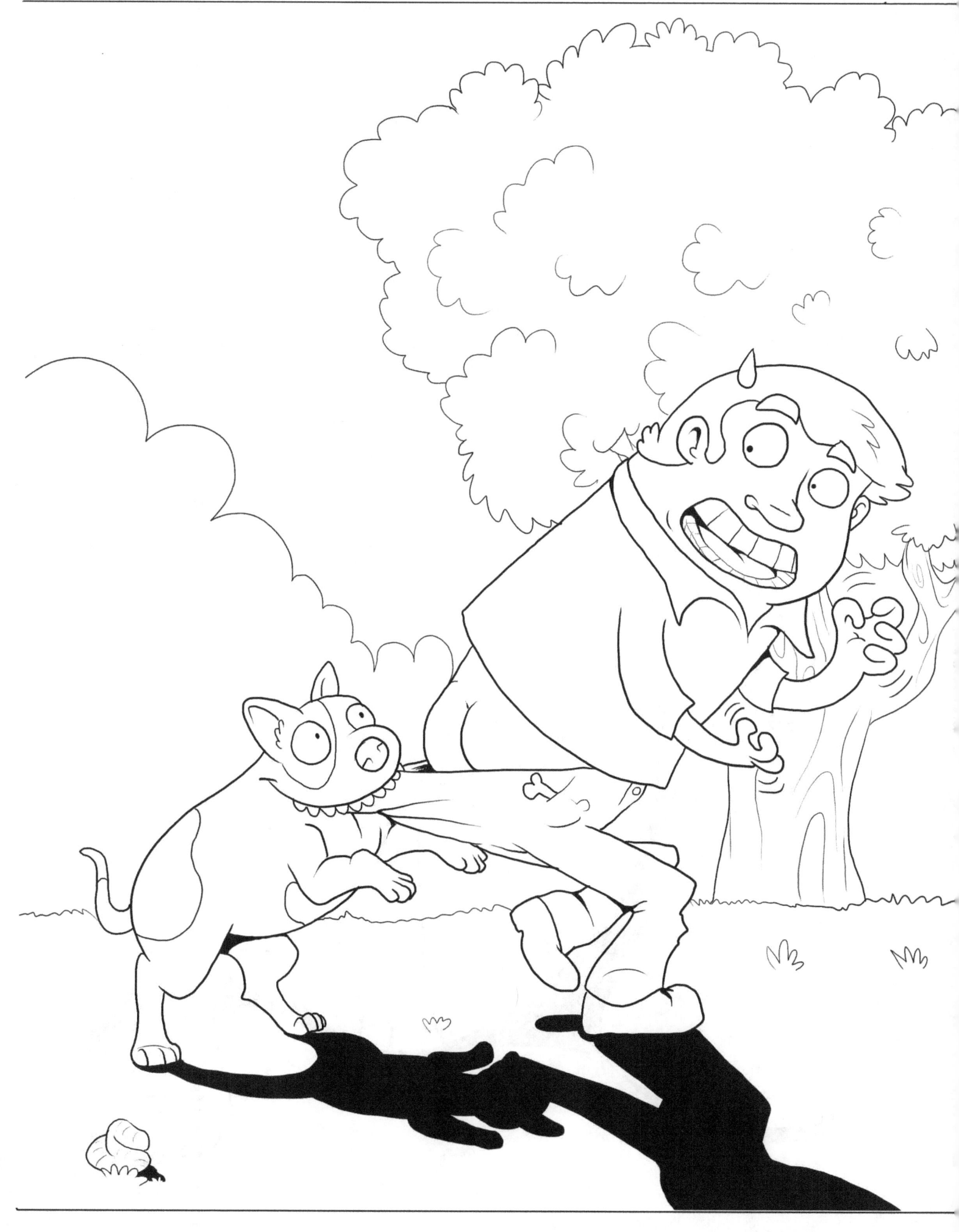

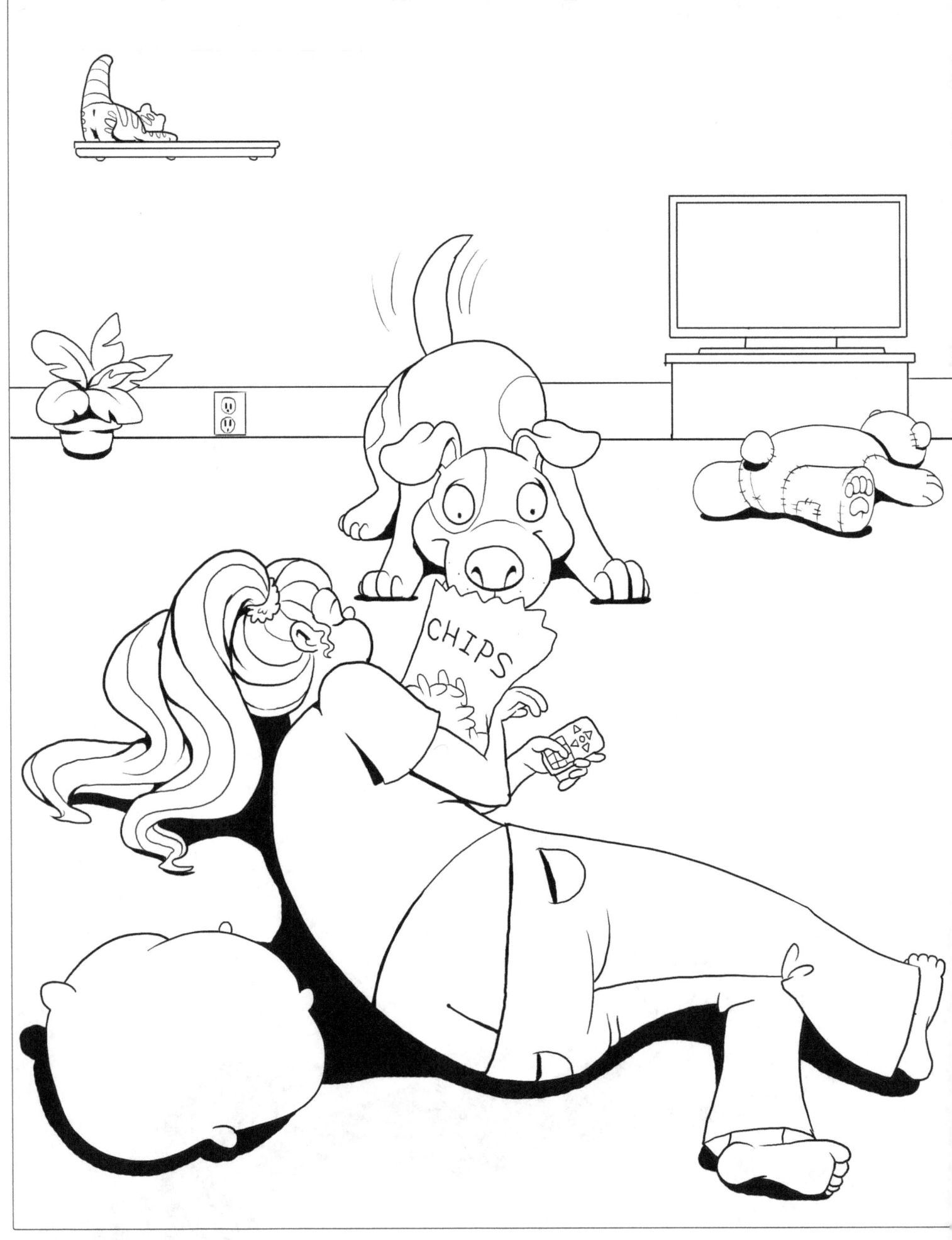

PLUMBER'S CRACK

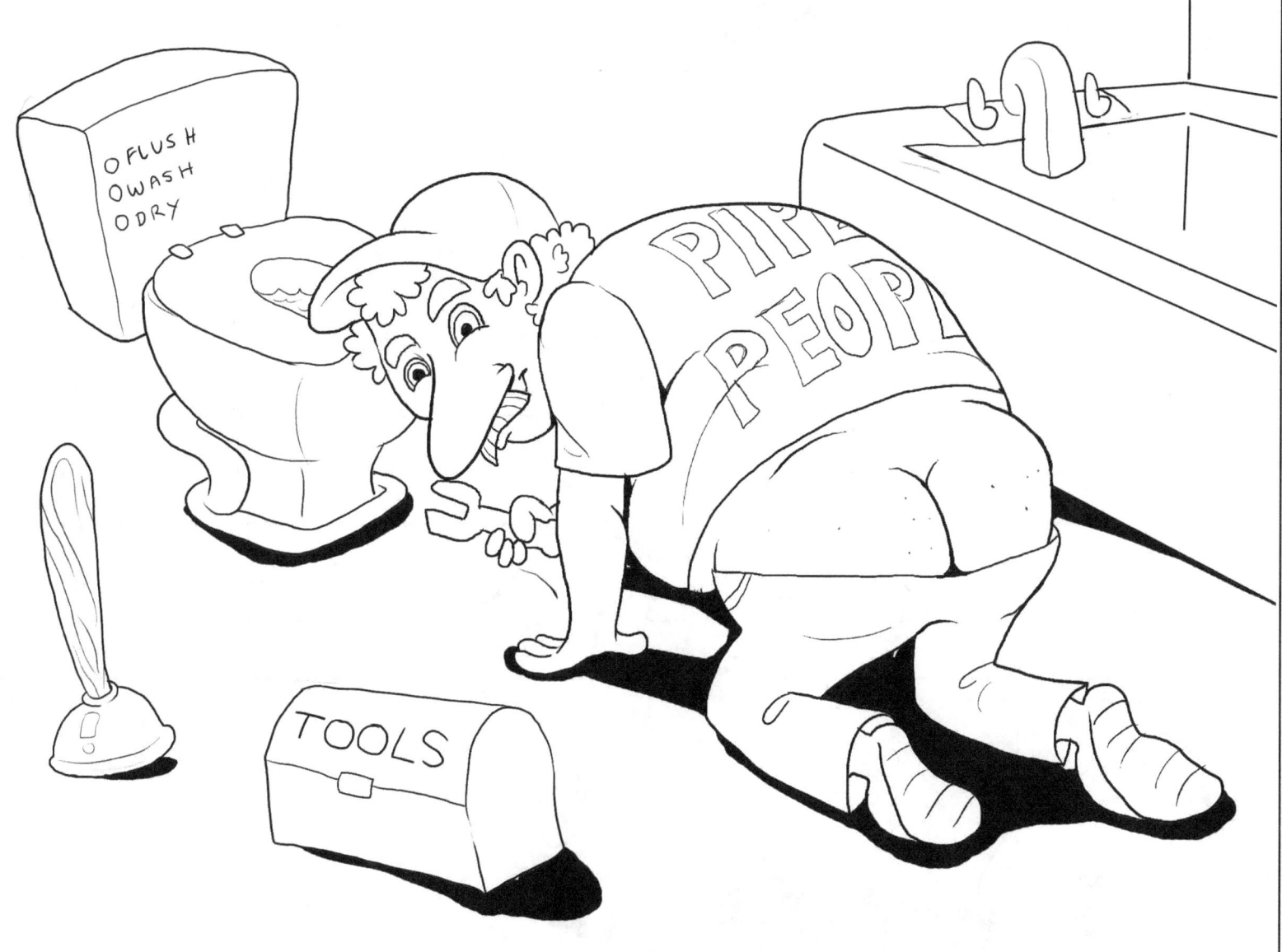

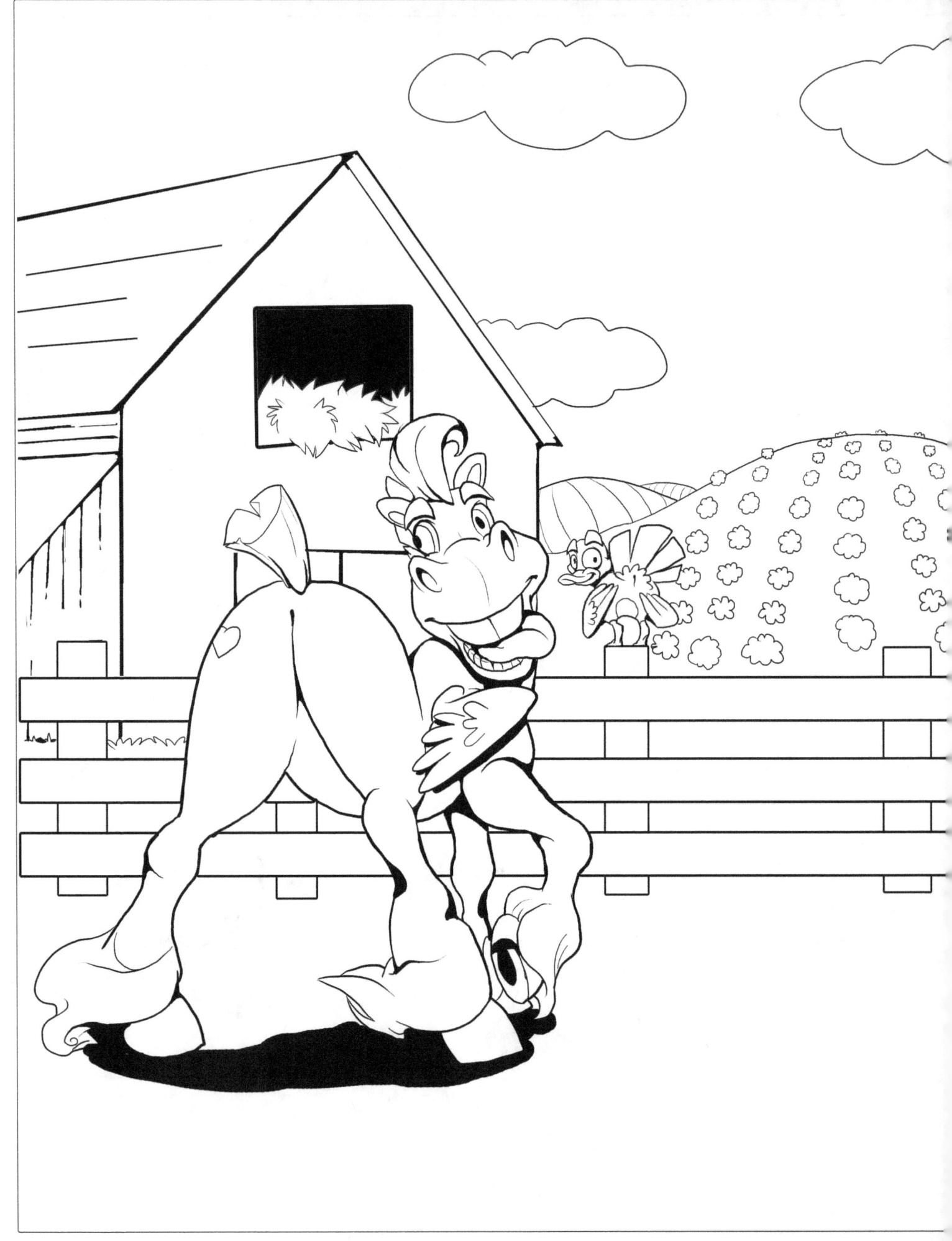

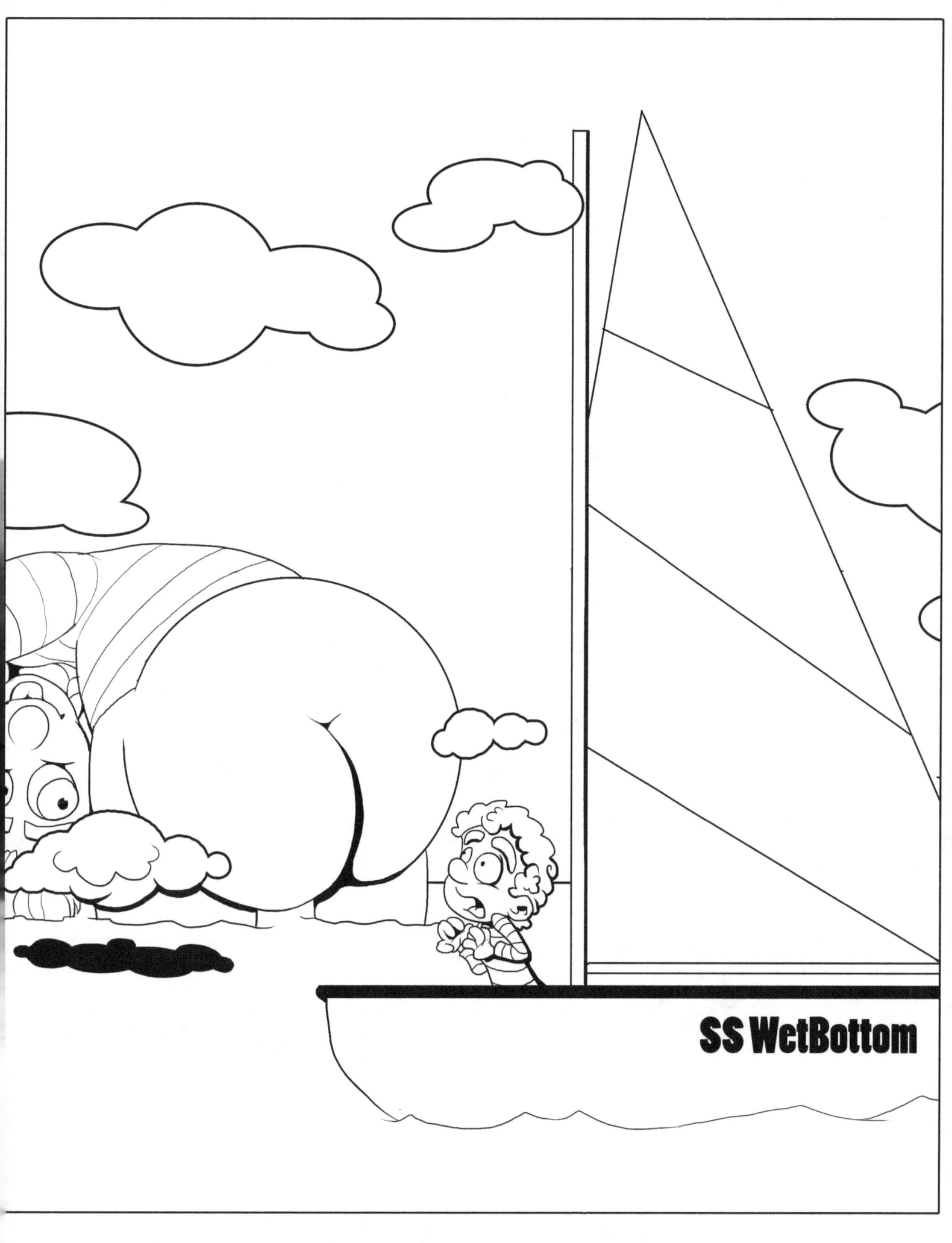

Peanut BUTTer

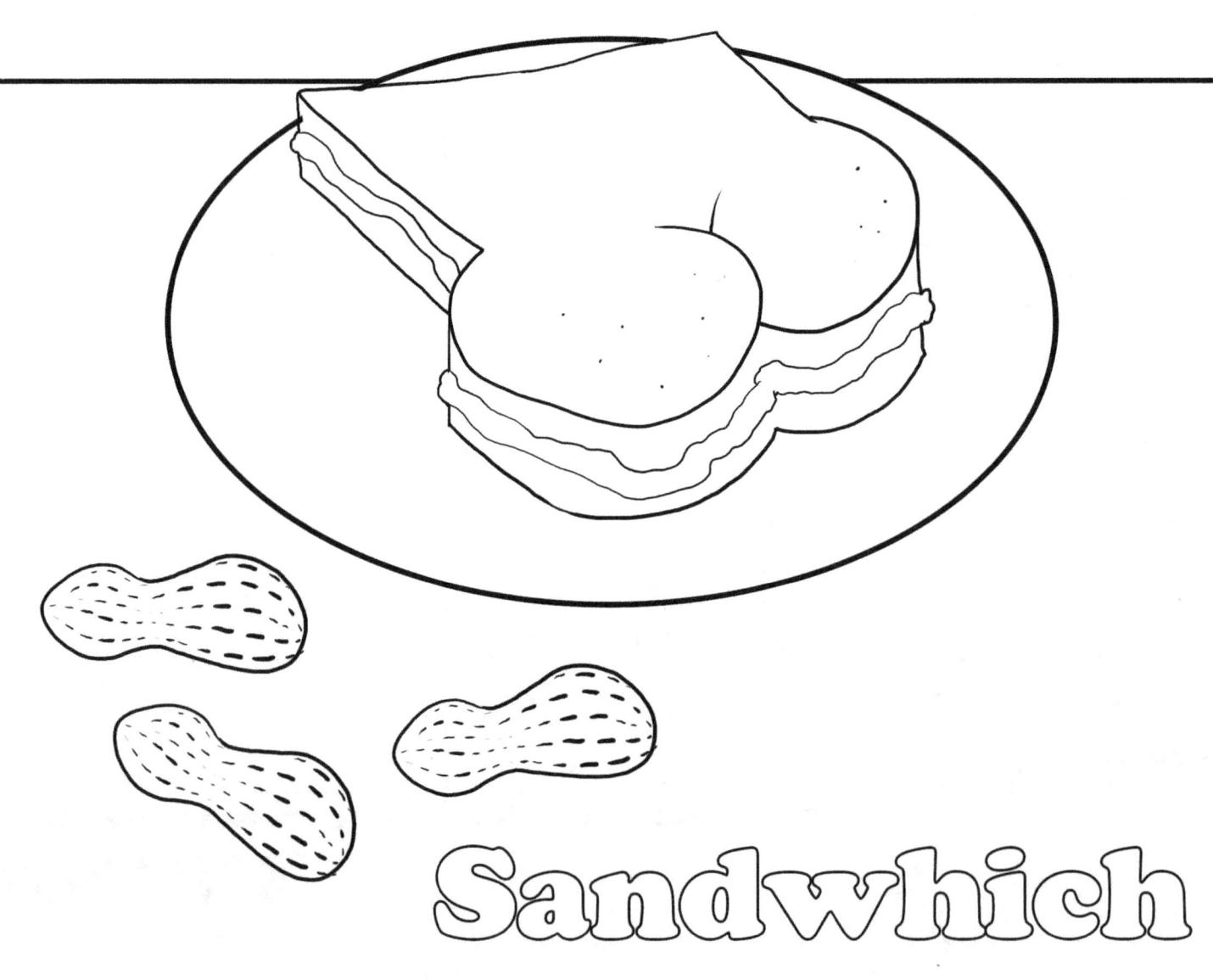

Sandwhich

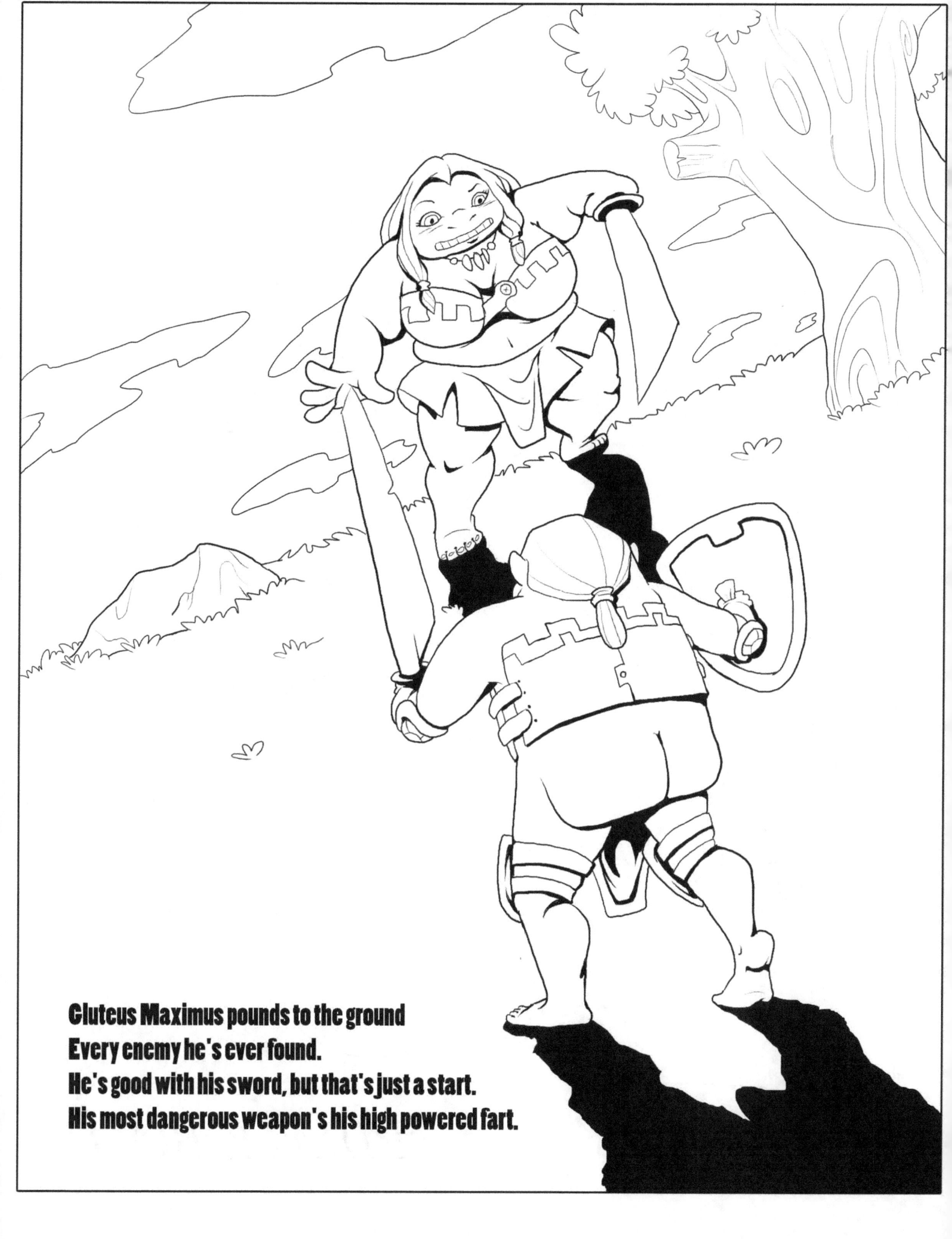

Gluteus Maximus pounds to the ground
Every enemy he's ever found.
He's good with his sword, but that's just a start.
His most dangerous weapon's his high powered fart.

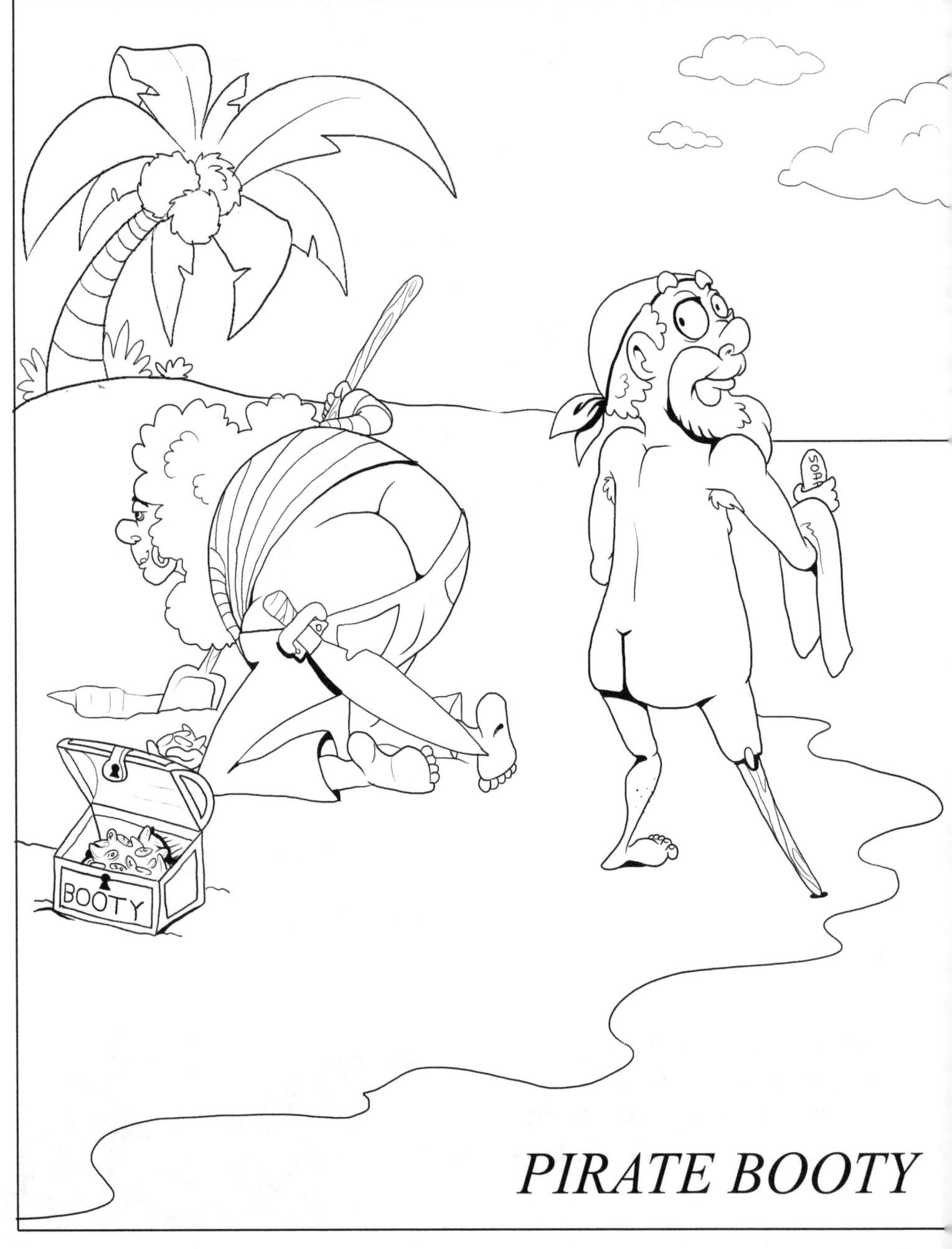

PIRATE BOOTY

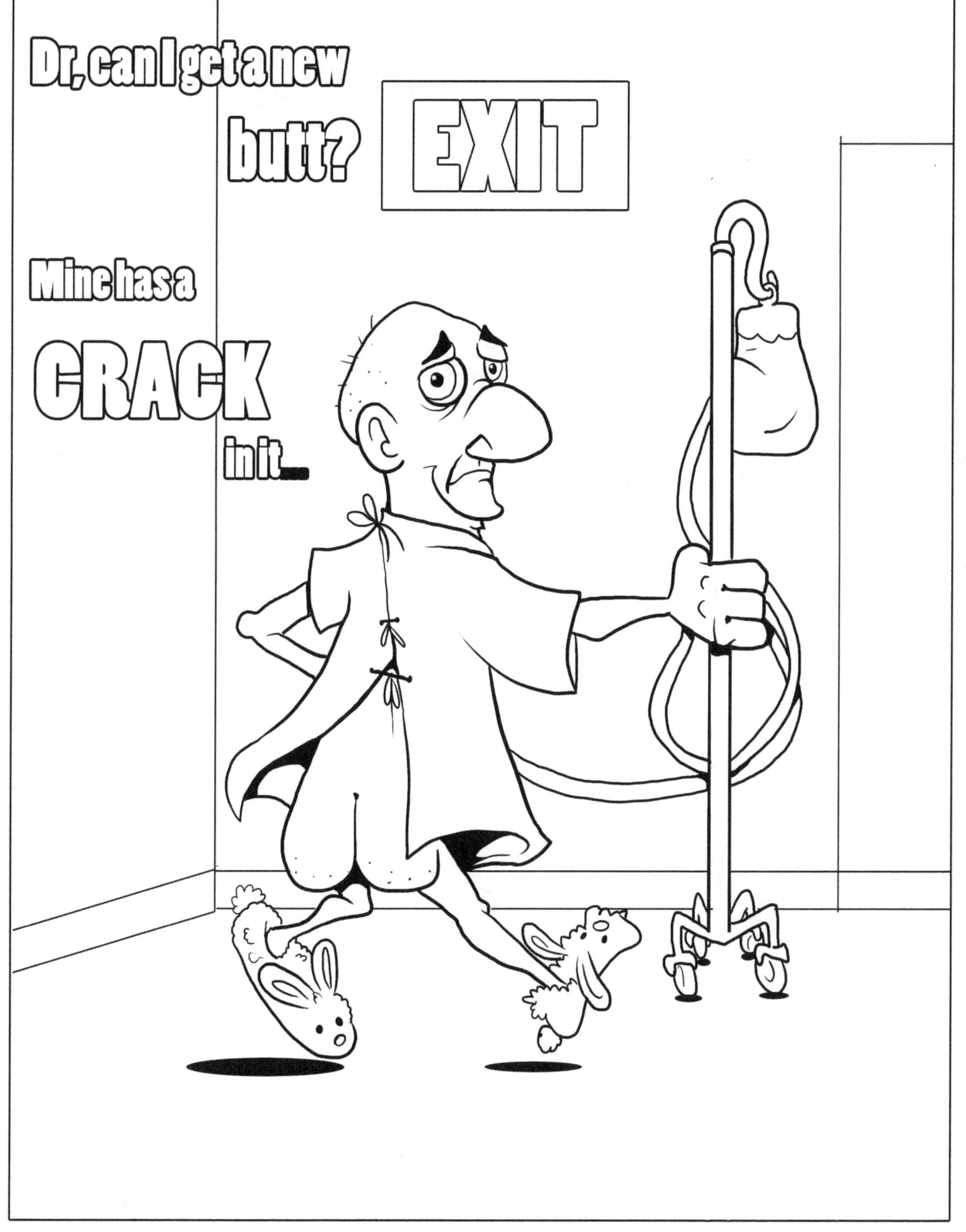

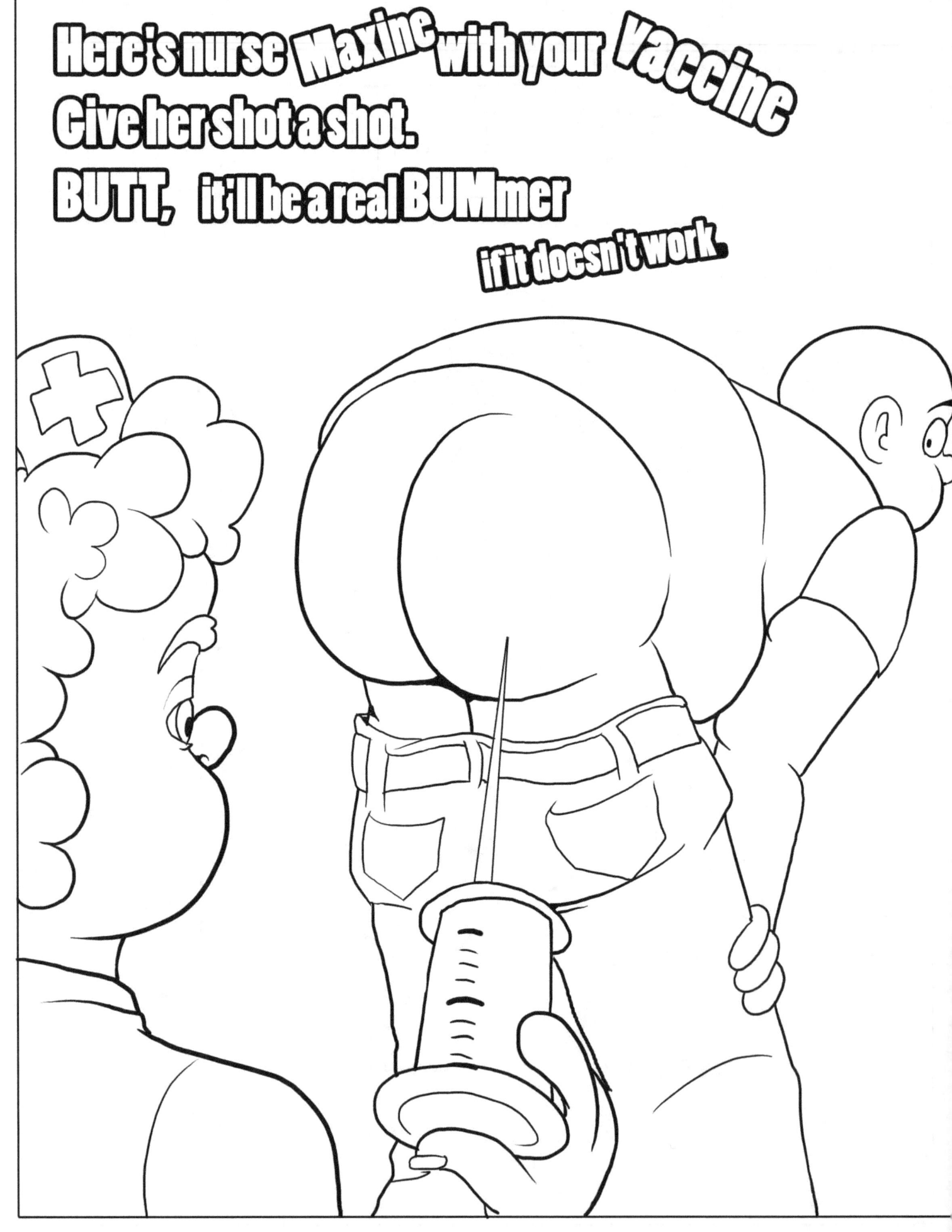

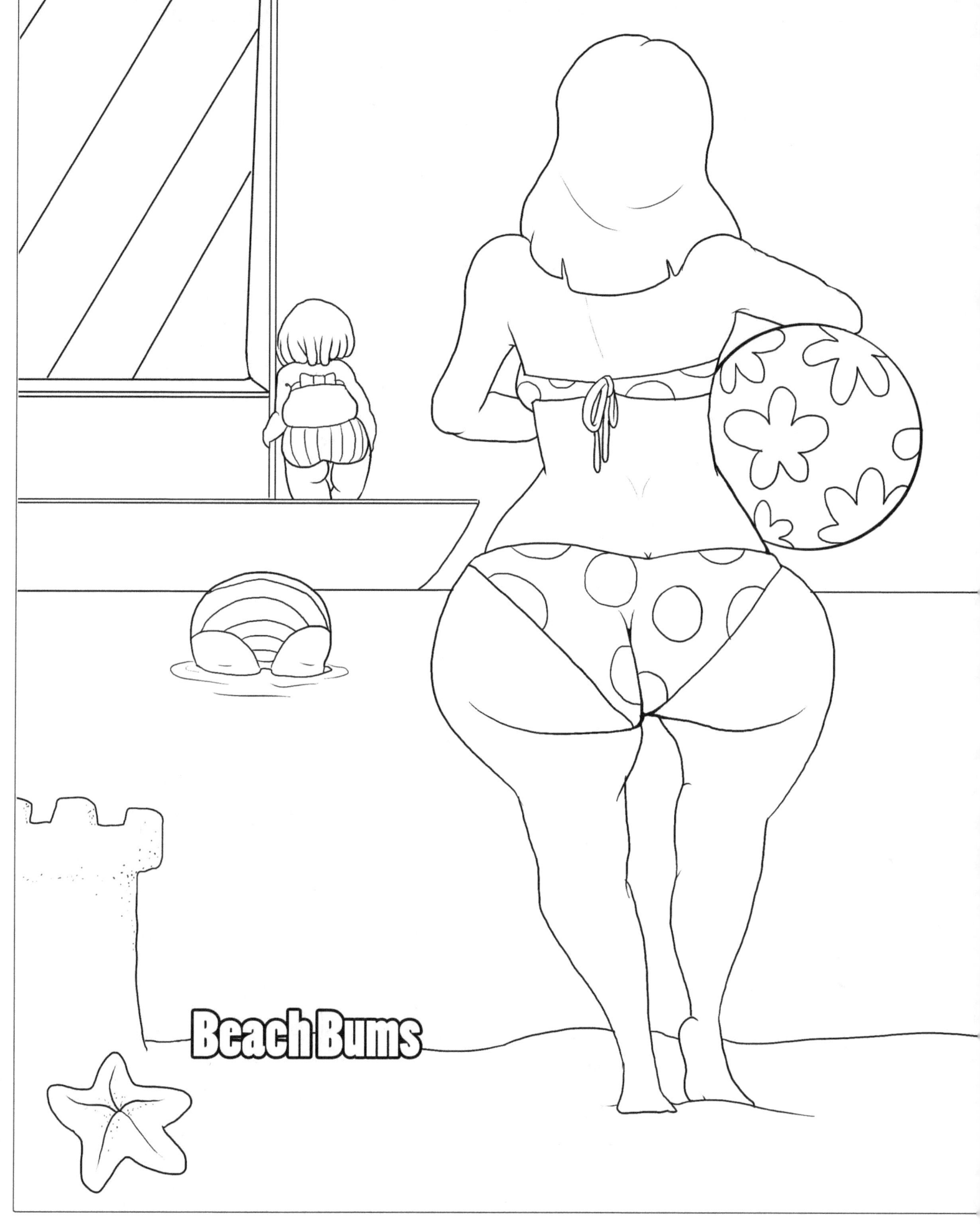

Beach Bums

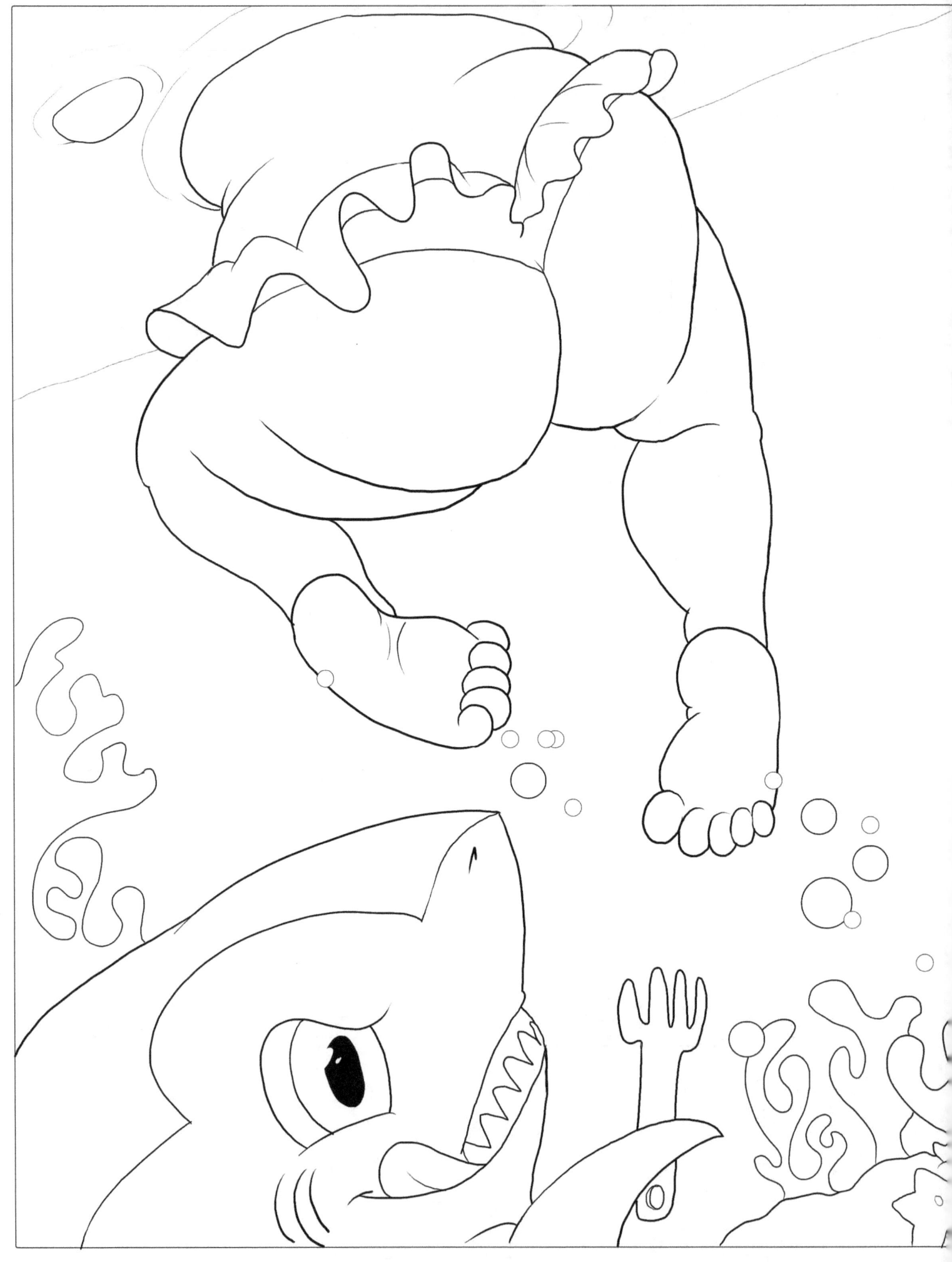

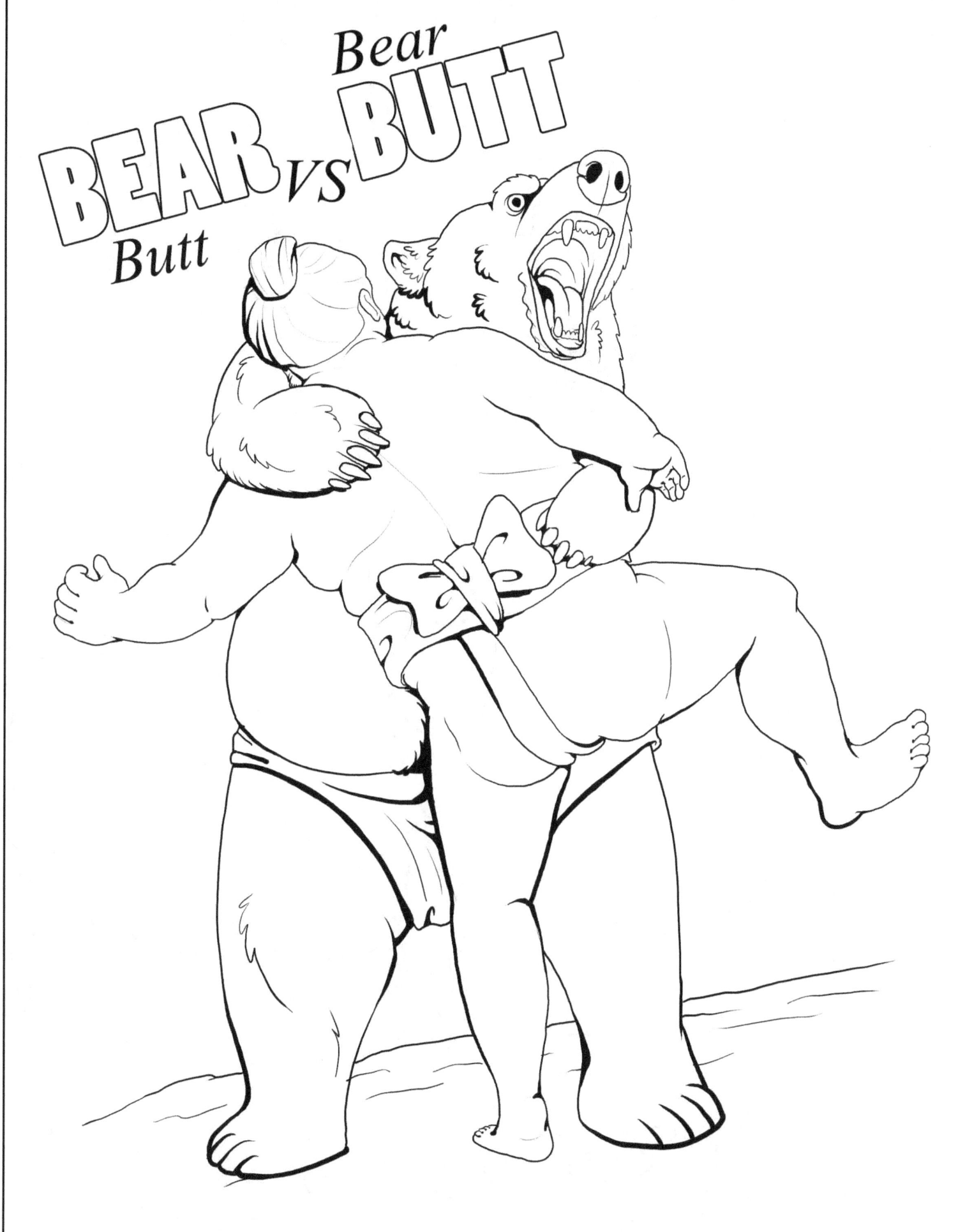

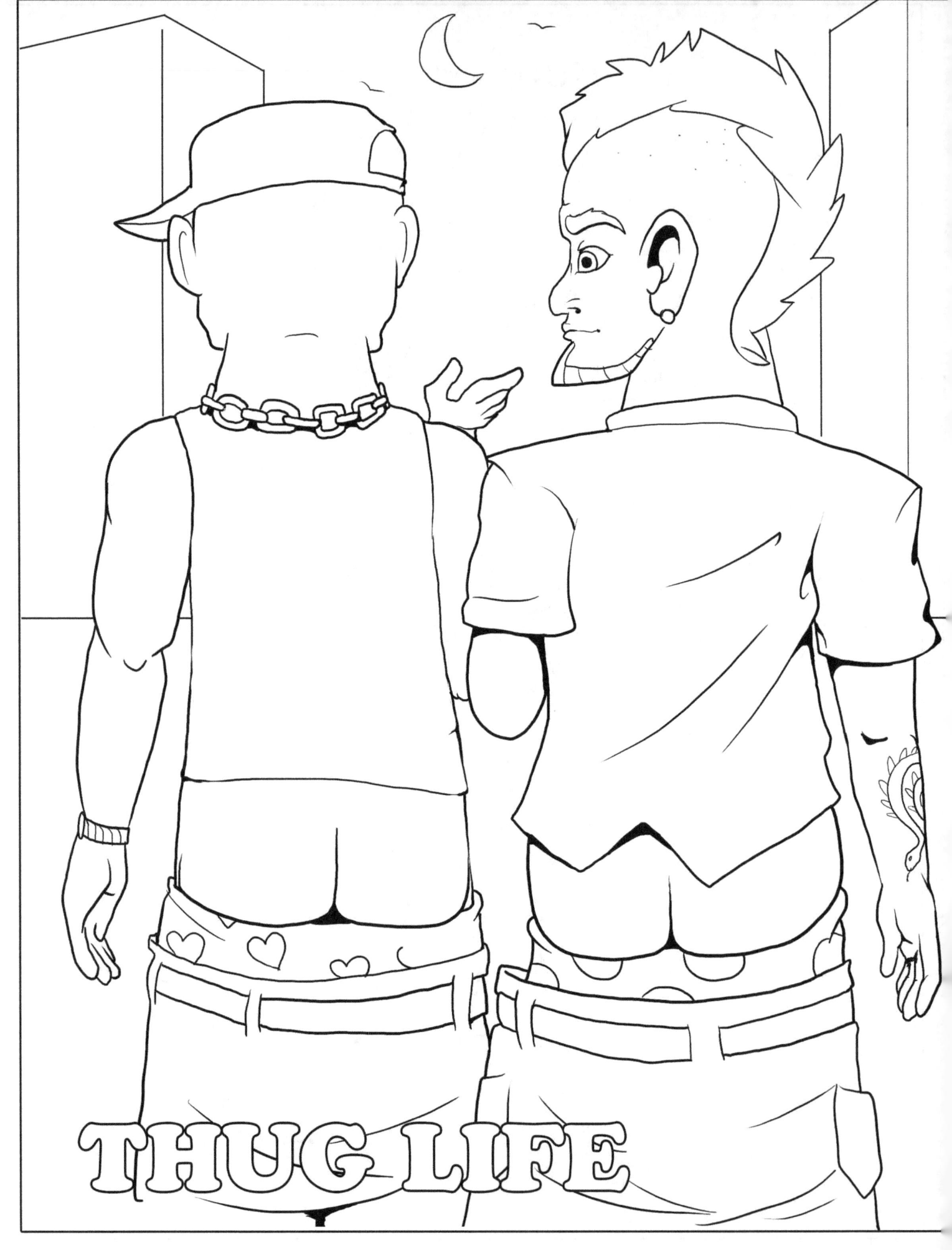

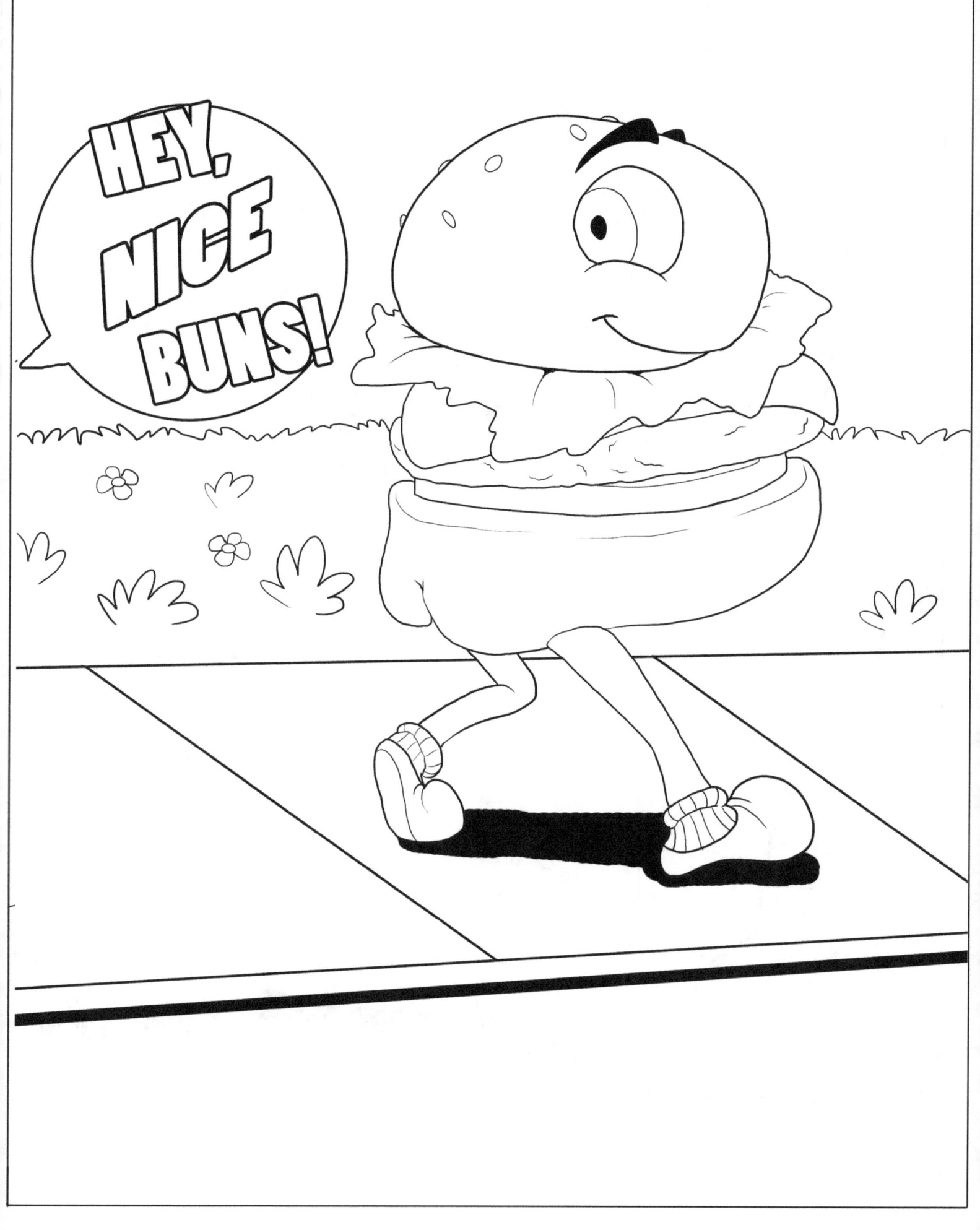

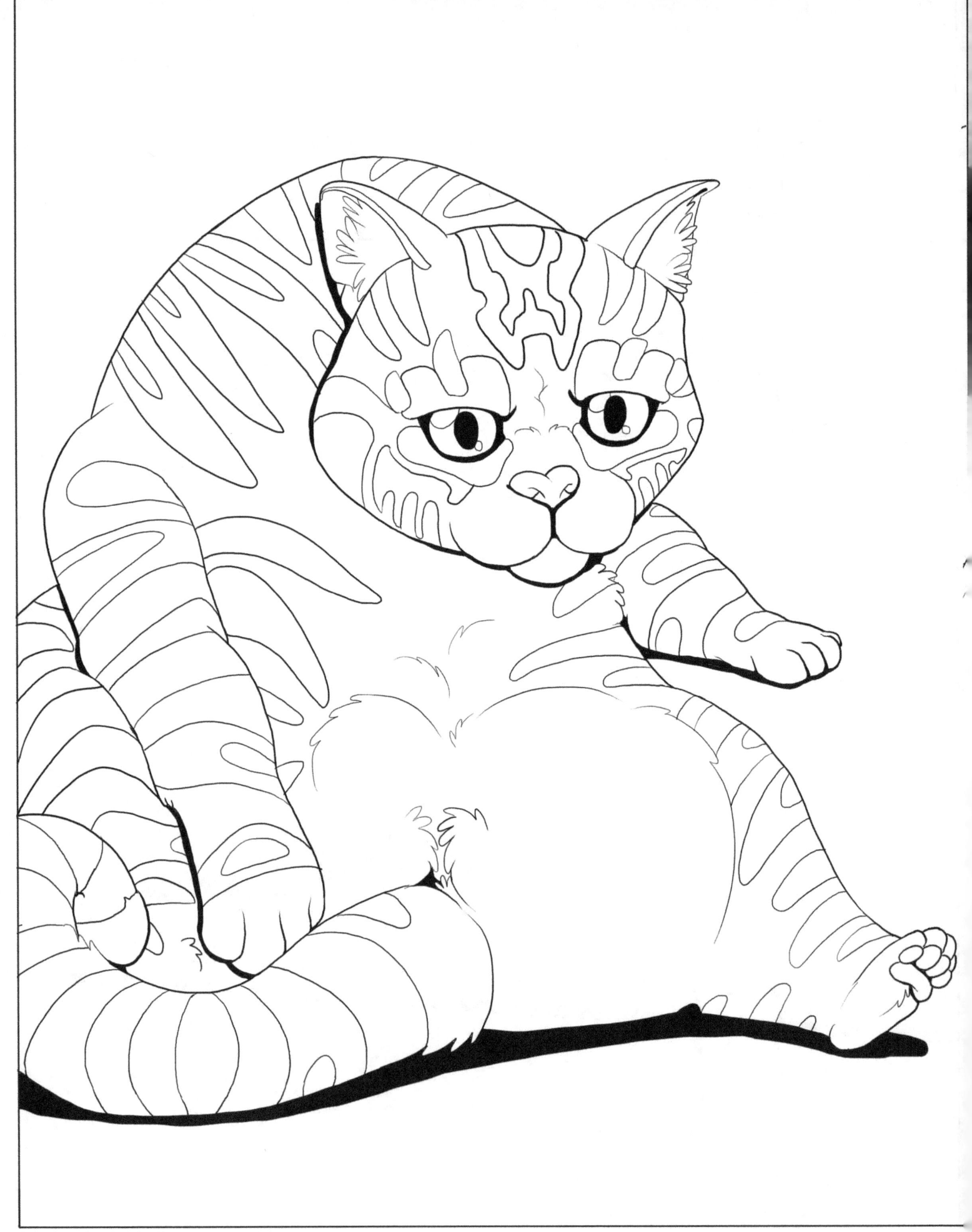

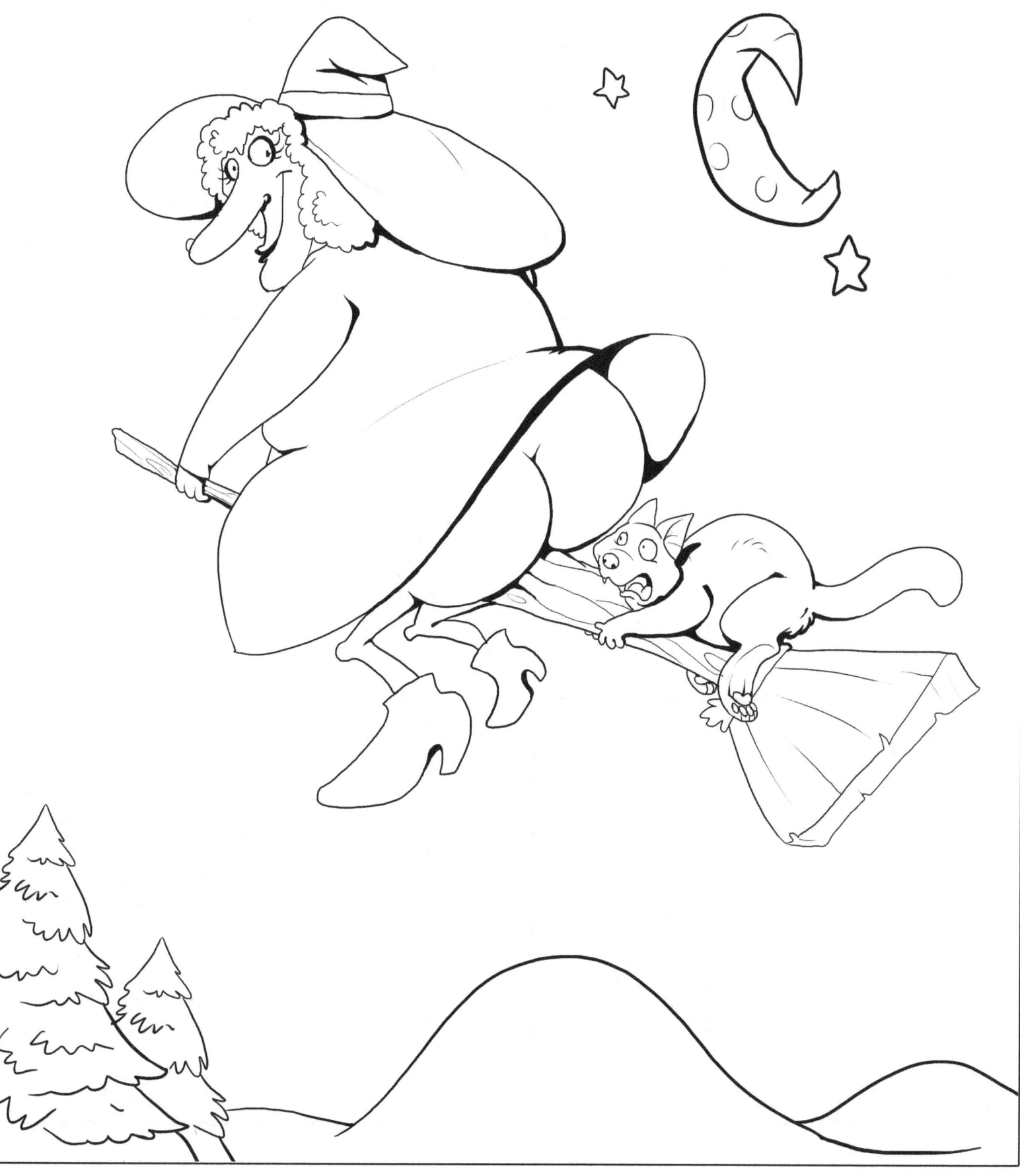

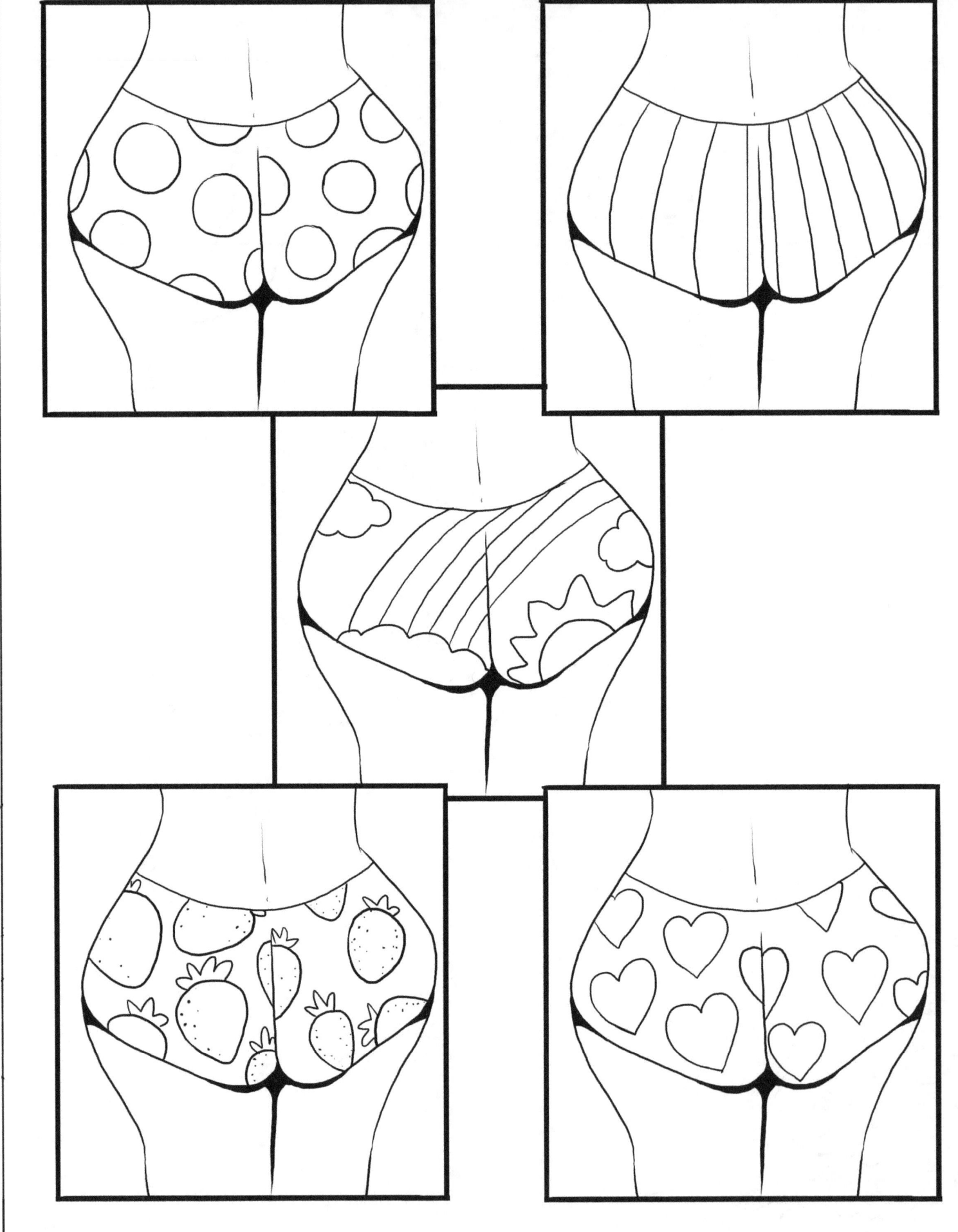

NOTHING BUT BUTTS
CROSSWORD PUZZLE

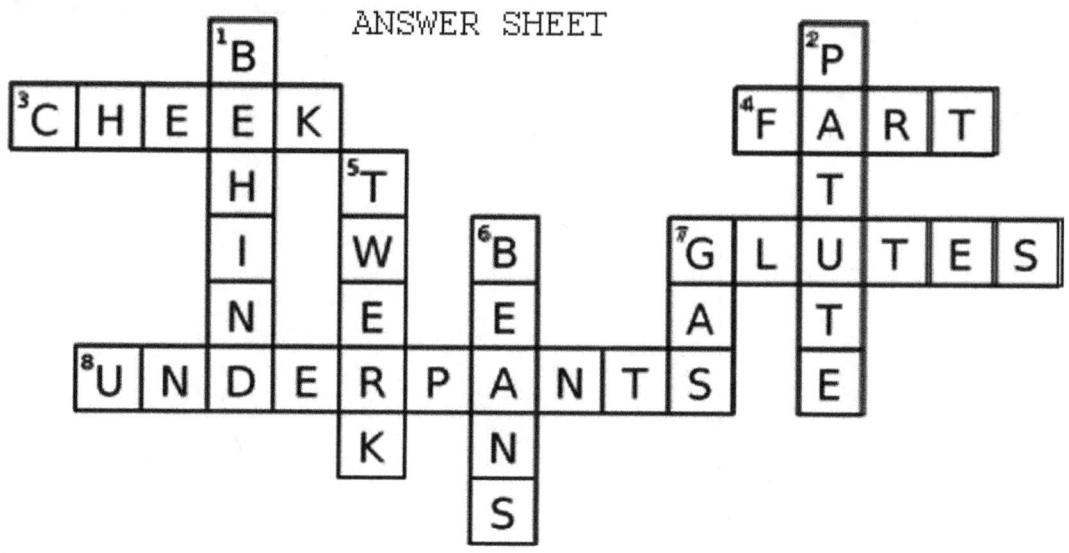

Down:
1. In back of the front
2. When your father farts - another word for butt
5. butt dance
6. Musical fruit
7. Stinky fuel

Across:
3. Turn the other one!
4. Music your butt makes
7. Butt muscle
8. Butt cover

MY POSTERIOR
How many words can you make using the letters found
in thie above statement? Write them below:

Post	MORE	REST
Most	YES	STEP
ROOSTER	STORY	STREP
MOP	STRIPE	TOY
STOP	STEM	MERRY
STOMP	TEMP	TRIP

...AND MANY MORE.

POOPY PUZZLE

Match the dookie to the bootie it came from.

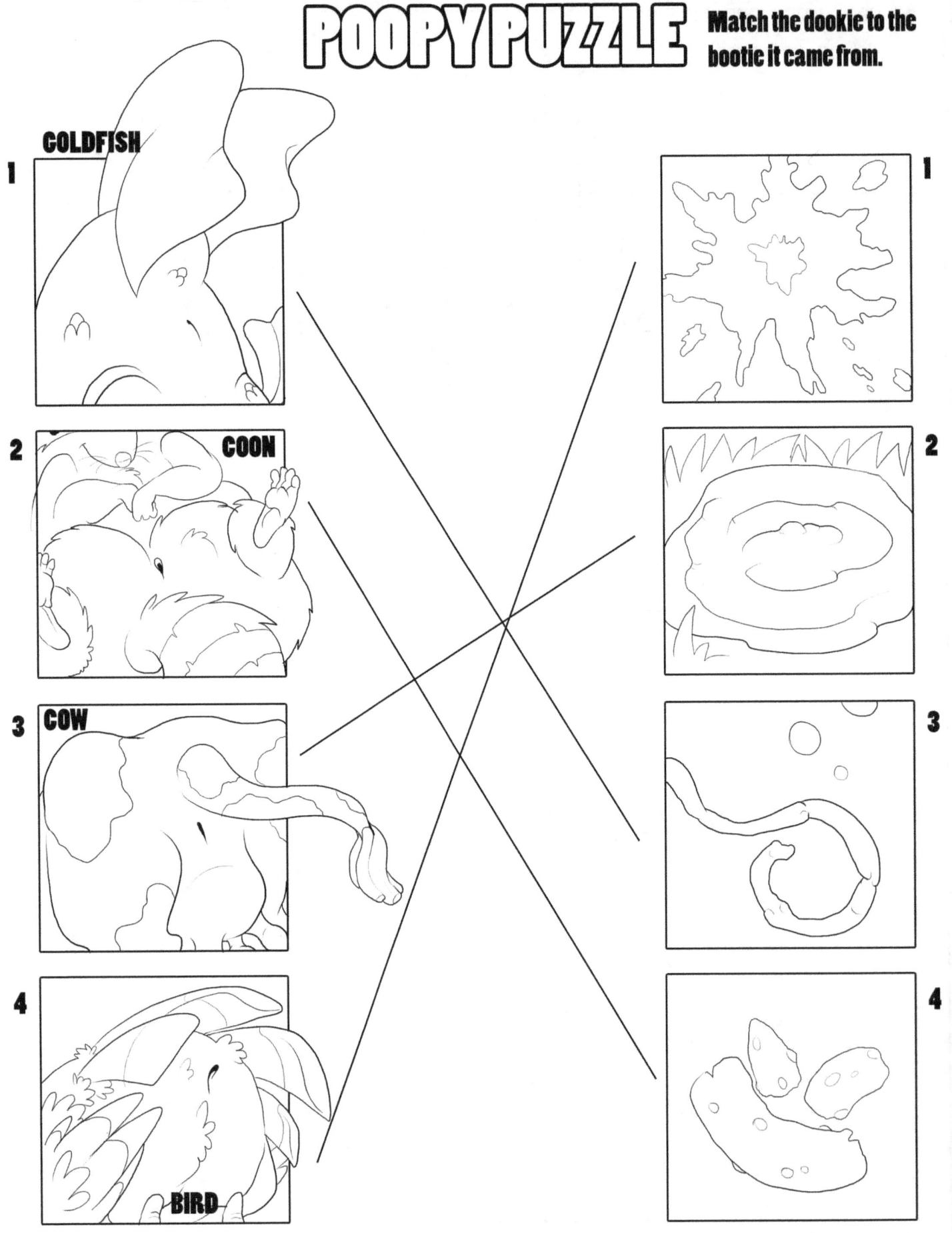